LET'S LOOK AT FEELINGS™

What I Look Like When I Am Angry

Heidi Johansen

The Rosen Publishing Group's
PowerStart Press™
New York

1

For Mamacita

Published in 2004 by The Rosen Publishing Group, Inc.
29 East 21st Street, New York, NY 10010

First Edition

Book Design: Kim Sonsky
Photo Credits: All photos by Maura B. McConnell.

Johansen, Heidi Leigh
What I look like when I am angry / Heidi Johansen.
p. cm. — (Let's look at feelings)
Includes index.
Summary: This book describes what different parts of the face look like when a person is angry.
  ISBN 1-4042-2508-0 (lib.)
1. Anger in children—Juvenile literature [1. Anger   2. Facial expression   3. Emotions]
I. Title   II. Series
  BF723.A4 J63 2004   2003-009455
  152.4'7—dc21

Manufactured in the United States of America

Contents

I am angry.

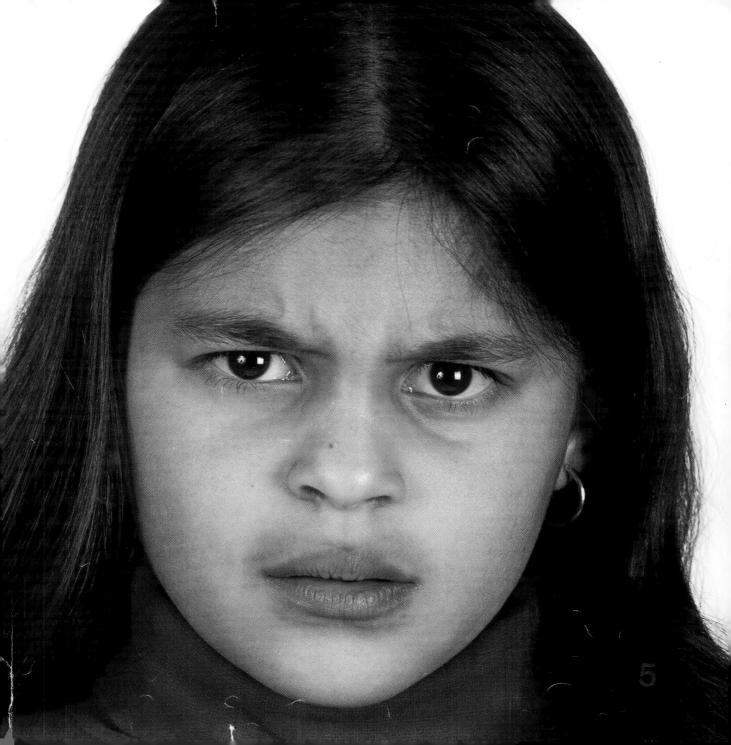

5

When I am angry my
eyebrows go down.

7

My eyes are small when I am angry.

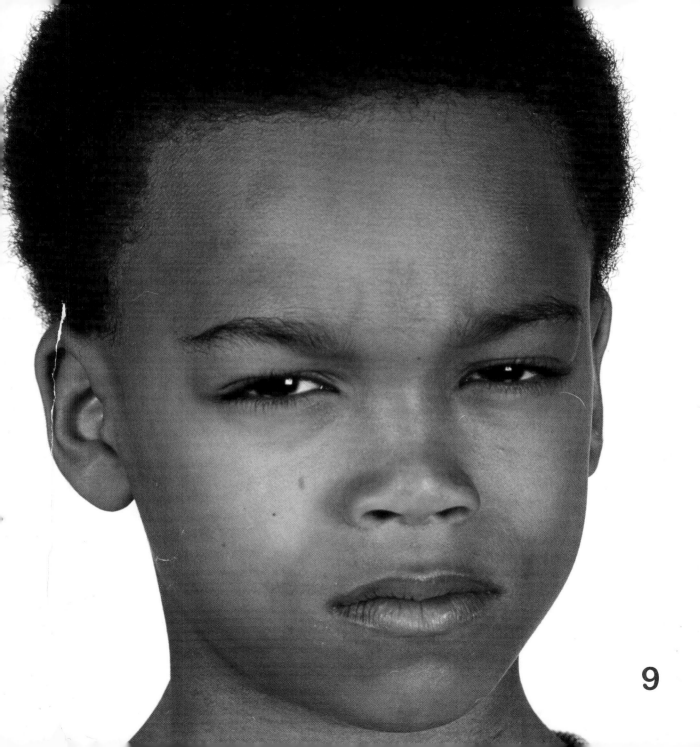

9

There are lines on my nose
when I am angry.

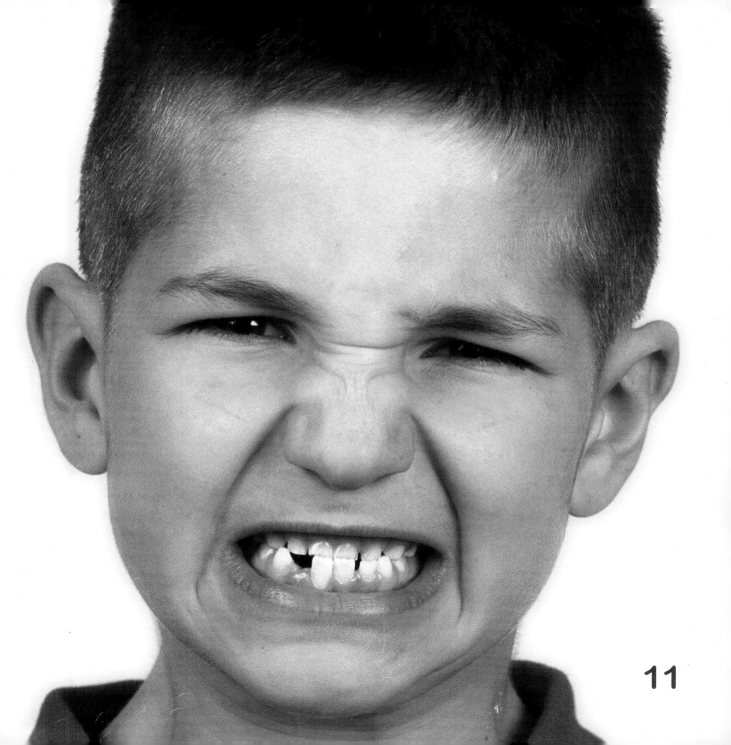

11

Both sides of my mouth go down when I am angry.

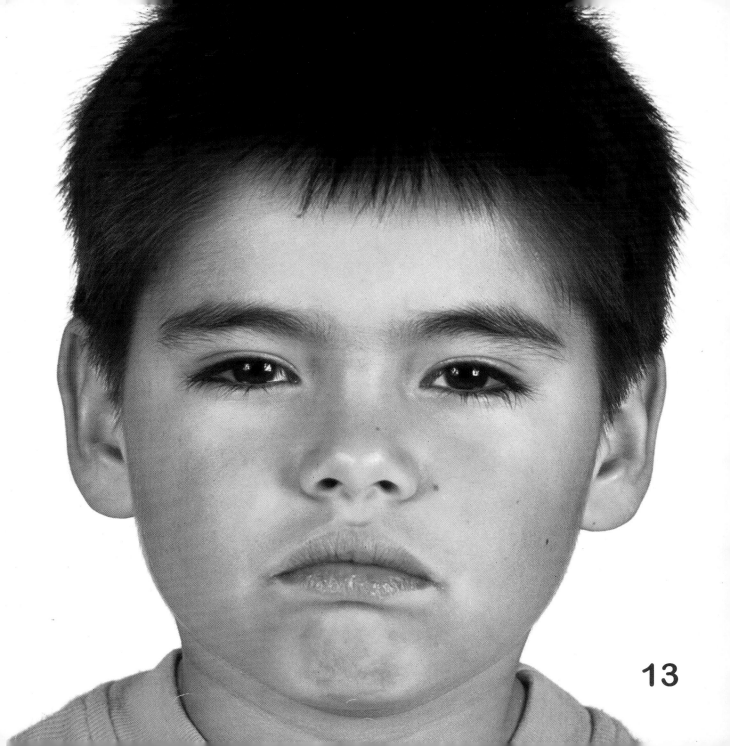

13

My mouth is closed tight when I am angry.

You can see my teeth when
I am angry.

My mouth opens in a yell
when I am angry.

18

When I am angry my face is red.

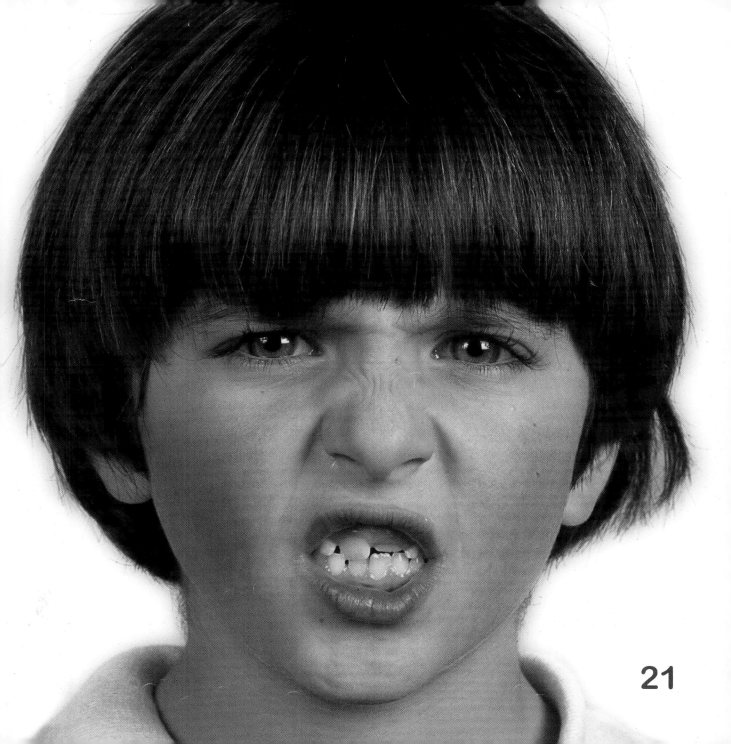

21

This is what I look like when
I am angry.

23

Words to Know

eyebrow

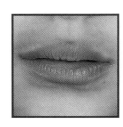

mouth

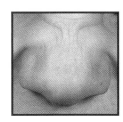

nose

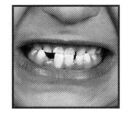

teeth

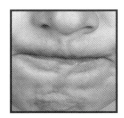

tight

Index

Web Sites

Due to the changing nature of Internet links, PowerStart Press has developed an online list of Web sites related to the subject of this book. This site is updated regularly. Please use this link to access the list:

www.powerkidslinks.com/llafe/angry/

24